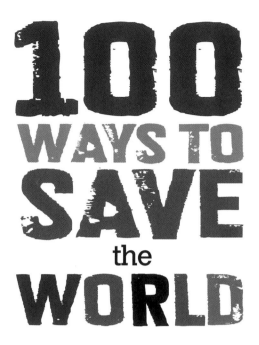

100 WAYS TO SAVE the WORLD

Johan Tell

Translated by Kevin Billinghurst

Foreword by

BILL McKIBBEN

GOLD ST.
PRESS

Published by Gold Street Press,
a division of Weldon Owen Inc.
415 Jackson Street
San Francisco, CA 94111
www.goldstreetpress.com

WELDON OWEN GROUP
Chief Executive Officer: John Owen
Chief Financial Officer: Simon Fraser

WELDON OWEN, INC.
President, Chief Executive Officer: Terry Newell
Vice President, International Sales: Stuart Lawrence
Vice President, Sales & Marketing: Amy Kaneko
Vice President, Publisher: Roger Shaw
Vice President, Creative Director: Gaye Allen
Art Director, Designer: Kelly Booth
Executive Editor: Mariah Bear
Associate Editor: Lucie Parker
Production Director: Chris Hemesath
Production Manager: Michelle Duggan
Color Manager: Teri Bell

Production Assistance: Hayden Foell

American Adaptation: Susan Sturgis

A WELDON OWEN PRODUCTION
© 2008 Weldon Owen Inc.

Library of Congress Control Number: 2008921961

ISBN 13: 978-1-934533-15-4

ISBN 10: 1-934533-15-7

10 9 8 7 6 5 4 3 2 1

Printed in China

First published by Bokförlaget Max Ström, Sweden

FOREWORD

This book sneaks up on you.

A glance at the title would make you think it was going to be one more list of things you could buy or small changes you could make to cut down on environmental destruction. And indeed there's plenty of that kind of advice, as there should be. We each need to think about the myriad little things we do each day, the endless ripples of our careless economic lives, the wake we leave behind us as we wander fairly thoughtlessly through the world. I just made dinner: could I have done it using half the energy? Quite possibly—there are tips in this book that will help all of us.

But it gives away its more powerful intent with the place it begins and ends. Political action is what we must engage in now if we are going to deal with the scale of the problem we face in the time that science allots us. I've spent the last year helping to organize almost 2,000 demonstrations in all 50 states about global warming. Our secret motto, as we did this work, became "Sure, screw in the new lightbulb. But then screw in the new federal policy." And if you talk to your political leaders, as this text politely suggests, and they don't listen, then "Screw in the new senator."

Many of the other great ideas in this book can also only be carried out by we, as opposed to you. Buying local food is a wonderful idea—but it presupposes the farmers market, and the set of legislative reforms that make local growing easier, and so on. Taking the bus is a necessary idea—but it presupposes the bus. If one exists, then hop on it; bend your schedule a few minutes either way to travel with your neighbors, as all of Europe does. If one doesn't exist—well, talk to your politician. And by talk, I mean organize so that he or she will listen to what you have to say.

Twenty years ago, when I wrote the first book for a general audience about global warming, we didn't quite understand just how fast this problem would break over our heads. We didn't guess that the ice caps would be already disintegrating, or the deserts spreading. Hence the urgency of the kind of changes this book proposes. They shouldn't be read, I think, as a collection of random ideas, to be adopted a few at a time. Instead, taken together, they imply a new way of thinking of ourselves. As citizens first, not as consumers. And as hedonists, not consumers: that is, as people who actually think about what makes us happy, as opposed to buying what we're told will fill us with joy. At some level, this is a book as much about saving your soul as saving your planet, and it should come as no surprise that they are connected.

Do not be discouraged. Or, when you become discouraged, for change is always a little hard, seek out others who are headed in the same direction. We need to be headed that direction together. We need a movement. And here are the ways you will recognize your fellow movers.

—Bill McKibben

PREFACE

The environment should be the dominant issue of our age.

The threats to our natural world overshadow everything else, because they will determine the future—for you and me and for everything living on this planet. Protecting the environment is a basic issue of survival, and the good news is that that insight is sinking in among the politically and economically powerful circles where crucial decisions are made.

The global environmental situation is serious, but far from hopeless. Climate issues have risen to the top of the agenda in recent years, but in reality it's a larger matter of changing the short-sighted and irresponsible way we manage our common natural heritage: the atmosphere, the seas, fishing, farming, forestry, energy, transportation, and all else that is affected by human activities.

In spite of the obvious problems there are enormous opportunities waiting to be addressed and huge profits to be won in the economic restructuring that we must now undertake. Because without that new alignment of environmental and economic priorities, the coming century will indeed be dire.

This book is about the many things that we can do as individuals in our daily lives, and that makes it an important source of inspiration. Together with leading researchers, Johan Tell reveals a plethora of small steps we can take without great effort, expense, or discomfort. Most of these suggestions are not only good for the environment; they're also good for your body, your soul, and your family budget.

The first step toward a sustainable future is simply to gain insight and understanding. From there, the step toward engagement and action is not particularly large or difficult. When we succeed in changing our everyday habits we also make fundamental improvements in our very way of life, and that opens the door to the deeper political, economic, and social change that must take place if we and our Earth are to survive together.

This book is one of the most stalwart and inspirational I have ever read during my long career in the environmental movement. It gives hope and encourages action. I hope Johan Tell's book will be read by many, and that readers will be moved to use these simple, concrete tips.

Only together can we create our common future, and most of the work is still before us. But without the kind of inspiration contained in the book you hold in your hand, the public will never come to the realization that the job is not to be left to experts. Every effort is important, and no effort is too small.

Come along!

Professor Lars Kristoferson
Secretary General, WWF Sweden

IT'S TIME.

That became clear to me on the 17th of December 2006, when I found spring flowers blooming in my garden in Sweden where there should have been snow. I reached a tipping point on that winter day, a moment when I realized that I had to begin taking a new path. I had visited a glacier hotel with no glacier left, seen barren desert where there should have been vegetation, and carried my children through floods in Asia. But now it became clear. The time had come. Time to do something for our overstressed environment, for our common future.

The relationship between extreme weather conditions and the greenhouse effect is now widely accepted by the vast majority of mainstream scientists.

As far back as 1896, Swedish chemist Svante Arrhenius became the first to speculate that changes in the levels of carbon dioxide in the atmosphere could substantially alter the Earth's surface temperature through what is now known as the greenhouse effect. More than a century later, the United Nations climate panel estimates that a doubling of atmospheric carbon dioxide levels over pre-industrial levels will raise Earth's average temperature 4 degrees Celsius, or 8 degrees Fahrenheit. Arrhenius figured it would take about 3,000 years, but he could foresee neither the world's population explosion nor the massive increase in per capita energy consumption that was coming.

Perhaps Arrhenius's most important contribution was to show that the principle of the greenhouse effect—if we burn too much fossil fuel, temperatures will inevitably rise—is not so complicated that it couldn't be understood a hundred years ago.

Yet it took until 2006 for the UN climate panel to convince its most skeptical members to accept the scientific findings that key heat-trapping gases in the atmosphere "have increased markedly as a result of human activities," and that the evidence of the climate's warming "is unequivocal, as is now evident from observations of increases in global average air and ocean temperatures, widespread melting of snow and ice, and rising global mean sea level."

Still there are doubters who point out that natural phenomena such as volcanic eruptions or sunspots could explain temperature variations, and that the climate has always gone through changes and will continue to do so. Greenland is often cited to prove the point, since farming was possible there until about 1450. Or that a cold spell at the turn of the 17th century meant that Shakespeare's contemporaries could ice skate on the Thames every winter, and Lake Superior stayed frozen until June. Or that the Vikings' grape-growing Vinland has become today's pine-forested Newfoundland.

But there are precious few left who still doubt that humans also affect climate. Even the Bush administration, which was initially reluctant to acknowledge climate change, admits that the greenhouse effect is a threat to species such as polar bears.

For the truth is that the American lifestyle, which is a looming disaster for the planet and which the rest of the world imitates more and more, is too dependent on automobiles, junk food and disposable rubbish. The average American spends more time driving a car than on vacation. Why shouldn't such a lifestyle be negotiable?

Apart from strange weather, another event in 2006 helped bring the environmental debate to the front burner: release of the Stern Review, in which UK economic advisor Sir Nicholas Stern presented a calculation of direct economic costs that we can expect to pay for climate change. The report estimates that global economic output will fall by at least 5 percent and perhaps as much as 20 percent unless strong measures are taken to reduce carbon emissions. Shifting to a low-carbon path could eventually benefit the economy by $2.5 trillion a year.

But the size of the Stern Review's price tag for climate change is perhaps less important than the simple fact that it is a price tag. Sir Nicholas, a well-tailored, well-educated, respected former chief economist at the World Bank, didn't scream out his message while chained to a tree and passing out pamphlets printed on recycled diapers. And his audience was not clad in hemp and podiatrically correct sandals, but included the world's leading economists, financiers and corporate leaders.

When environmental warnings begin to encompass the global economy, the market begins to listen. Suddenly there was a wider discussion of green capitalism, smart growth, and how companies can strive to be climate neutral by reducing carbon emissions and compensating for the rest by purchasing emission rights or planting trees.

Environmental issues leaked out of musty community center meeting halls and into corporate boardrooms to the rustle of hastily assembled theme issues of *Newsweek* and *The Economist*.

Finally, it seemed that the environmental movement and the market were moving in the same direction.

Beyond the importance of bringing market forces to bear on climate change, the Stern Review highlighted the crucial role of politicians. The report was conducted under a mandate from the British government, and Tony Blair called it "the most important document about the future I have read since becoming prime minister."

There is little doubt that external factors led to Blair's ordering the report. To at least some extent, he chose to elevate environmental issues because they are important to the people of the nation.

That's why the most important thing you can do for the environment is not to switch to a green car or recycle your newspapers or buy low-energy lightbulbs. The most effective way to make a difference is to make it clear to your politicians that you want to see environmental concerns addressed at the highest levels.

Democracy is not just a matter of going out to vote every few years when an election rolls around. Participating in democracy means maintaining a dialog with those in power.

But while you communicate with elected officials, there are a lot of small choices you make that add up to big impacts—both directly through reduced energy consumption and waste, and indirectly by sending the right signals to politicians at all levels of government so they know they have the support they need to push for change.

Coming back from picking mushrooms in the woods, I pass a barn. The cows inside are belching methane gas. A dairy herd can be seen as a symbol for our problems with greenhouse gases. It's not the gases themselves—in addition to carbon dioxide the Kyoto Protocol addresses methane, nitrous oxide, hydrofluorocarbons, perfluorocarbons, and sulphur hexafluoride—the problem is the amount of them. These gases are crucial to retaining the heat we need to live on Earth and to spreading out the heat we receive from the sun so that we have tolerable temperatures from the equator almost up to the poles. But an excess of greenhouse gases will cause temperatures to rise. Spring flowers bloom in December, because we burn too much fossil fuel and have too many belching cows. It's that simple.

The Kyoto Protocol is an international treaty that came into effect on February 16, 2005 and has been signed and ratified by 172 nations, though not the United States. It calls for a 5 percent reduction in greenhouse gases from 1990 figures by 2008–12.

If 5 percent sounds like a small amount, it could be because 5 percent is just that—too little. No serious observer believes that that reduction is enough to stop global warming.

We're going to have to make greater changes in our lives.

The first step is to recognize that we can't consume ourselves out of this crisis. Even if you always make the right environmental choices, buying more won't help. You'll have to learn to consume less. Get used to the idea that pretty much everything you use directly or indirectly contributes to carbon emissions.

Are there any positive signs? Of course there are.

- Many countries around the world have developed strategies to replace fossil fuels with renewables.
- More and more politicians are putting environmental arguments on the agenda.
- The global population is growing more slowly than earlier predictions suggested. A few years ago, the UN was predicting a 2050 population of more than 12 billion, but that figure has been reduced to 9 billion.
- The Kyoto Protocol's goals may be modest, but signatures from more than 170 countries indicate that most of the world takes global warming seriously.

It's important to keep these positive signs in mind during a time when catastrophe warnings are constantly in the news. We all need to keep making the right small environmental decisions while we encourage politicians and corporate leaders to make the right big ones. Don't believe the pessimists who say it doesn't matter what we do as individuals. They're wrong. And don't forget what former Vice President Al Gore said in his film *An Inconvenient Truth*: "The danger is that people will go from denial to despair without stopping in between to ask themselves what action they can take."

It's time to recognize that we have to find new ways to think. If global warming is to be managed, we can no longer treat the planet's limited reserves of fossil fuel the way we have since the dawn of the Industrial Age. The oil and gas that is left in the ground needs to be conserved for higher-value uses than heating buildings and moving people and goods from one place to another. It's time to recognize that we need to make a leap beyond oil dependency. Or as Saudi Arabian Sheikh Zaki Yamani said: "The Stone Age didn't end for lack of stone, and the oil age will end long before the world runs out of oil."

Let's prove him right.

It's time.

CALL A POLITICIAN. You can't change the world by yourself. On the other hand, no politician can save the world without you. Bringing change to environmental policies may require regulation and prohibitions, or economic measures like emissions trading. Either way, widespread popular support is essential.

That's where your phone call comes in. Email is also a great way to make yourself heard, and many politicians are on the web, where other visitors may see your comments. Or why not write a good, old-fashioned letter?

Even if you believe that the Earth can be saved only by large, international political decisions, you can start by getting in touch with local politicians. They interact with parties and other politicians, and many are aiming for higher office. You just might be talking to a future state official, and it's not far from there to Washington and beyond.

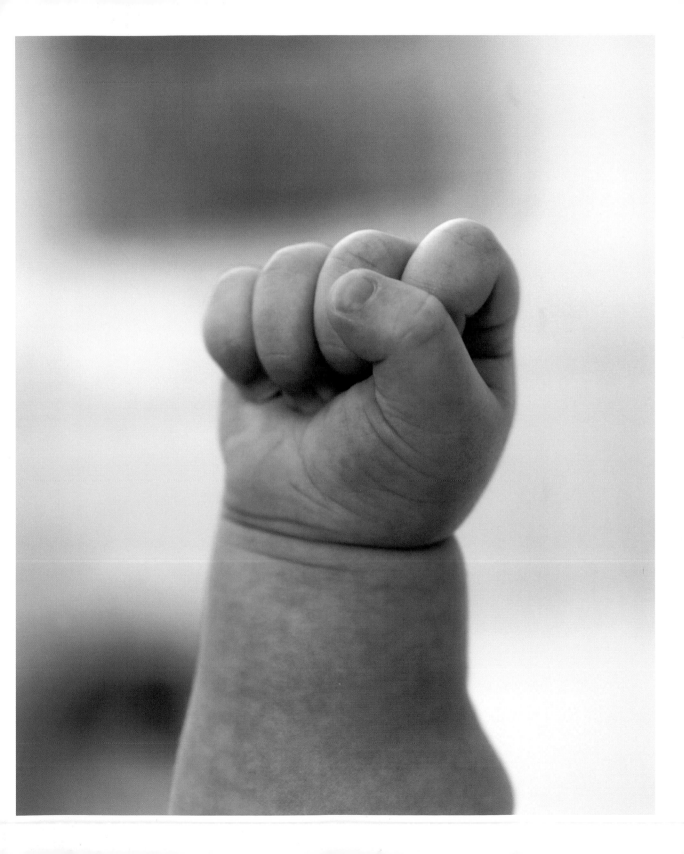

2

BUY QUALITY. Shop for fewer, better products that will last longer. Enormous amounts of resources are wasted on poor-quality items that quickly get broken, wear out, or simply go out of fashion. A good pair of shoes should last ten years, a car twenty, a piece of furniture two—generations, that is.

Don't buy things that won't last. Don't buy things you'll get tired of. Only throw things away when they're worn out. You might have to pay more, but you'll pay a lot less often.

3

SINK THOSE PIRATES. When you buy unauthorized copies of name-brand goods, there's a good risk you'll be buying a product made by underage workers in sweatshop factories.

You may or may not think designer labels are worth the extra money, but global companies at least face a certain amount of pressure to maintain their images and not be exposed as villains. Most big companies publish ethics codes, and they have to respect minimum wage laws, environmental controls, and negotiated working conditions. Pirates can't be held responsible for anything.

4

UNDERSTAND WHAT YOU BUY. If the content label on a product lists mostly compounds that you're not familiar with, there's a good chance that they aren't the best things for your body or for the ecosystem.

5

TAKE THE TRAIN. Rail travel is a clear environmental winner over airplanes and cars. Some estimates put carbon dioxide releases from air travel at ten times as much per passenger mile as a train. Others say it's three hundred times as much. It all depends on the distance traveled, since airplanes pollute most on take-off and landing. Of course, there's also a big difference depending on whether the train runs on electricity from renewable sources or from fossil fuel.

Also, the train is also simply a more civilized way to travel. You can meet people, sleep, work, or enjoy a drink.

CONNECT THE DOTS. It's not a wild exaggeration to say that everything contributes to global warming. Pretty much all production releases carbon dioxide, as does all motorized transportation. And that's especially true of all those gadgets that run on electricity, whether from the power lines or from batteries, as well as anything powered by diesel, gas, or ethanol.

You don't need to learn how everything works. But a basic understanding of how different products are connected to energy consumption will help you figure out where you can save. To put it into context, let's say you'd like to cut your personal carbon output by 500 pounds. You could:

- Replace nine 60-watt standard lightbulbs with low-energy compact fluorescent lights. During the life of these long-lasting lamps you'll save more than 500 pounds of carbon.
- Replace 750 miles of car travel with bicycling.
- Cut your driving speed from 68 mph to 55 mph for 3,700 miles.
- Replace a two-stroke outboard boat motor with a four-stroke. In just 30 hours of running time you'll save 500 pounds of carbon.
- Replace the meat in one of every four dinners with legumes. A family of four will save 500 pounds of carbon in a year.

If none of these suggestions is quite right, you can plant 21 trees. Your trees will absorb about 500 pounds of carbon a year, and they should keep working for at least another forty years or so.

To get a clear picture of how lifestyle choices contribute to the greenhouse effect, check out the US Environmental Protection Agency's Personal Emissions Calculator at www.epa.gov/climatechange/emissions/ind_calculator.html.

7

SEE NATIVE WILDLIFE. Ecotourism doesn't have to mean traveling abroad. Environmentally themed destinations abound throughout the United States. Take a boat trip to the San Juan Islands off the Washington coast to watch whales. Or go bird watching in the Everglades, or sea kayaking off the Maine Coast. Visit one of the more than 50 national parks.

Take a weekend trip by bus or train, and simply check into a hotel, then go paddling in a lake or take a hike and see where you wind up.

8

EAT SUSTAINABLY RAISED MEAT. Americans adore their meat, but that love affair—200 pounds consumed per person in 2005—takes a toll on the environment, with pollution from factory farms, health threats from drug-resistant bacteria, and consumption of fossil fuels to raise and transport animals. A 2005 study published in the International Journal of Agricultural Sustainability calculated the hidden costs of industrially farmed meat in the United States at somewhere between $5.7 billion and $16.9 billion a year.

A growing number of US farmers are turning to more environmentally friendly methods of raising meat. Pasture-raised cattle, for example, not only get to spend their lives outdoors eating grass as nature intended, but they also produce healthier beef than their factory-farmed counterparts, with less total fat and calories and more beneficial omega-3 fatty acids. Such meat costs more than industrial alternatives, it's true, but US consumers tend to eat too much meat anyway. Nutritionists consider a serving size of beef as three ounces—about the size of a deck of cards.

SWITCH ELECTRIC COMPANIES. US electrical power is largely generated by fossil fuels—coal, oil, and natural gas. If we are to substantially reduce our emissions of greenhouse gases, this will need to change. If you can, choose an electricity provider offering energy from renewable sources. If switching providers isn't an option, consider purchasing renewable energy certificates. For more details, check with the Department of Energy's Green Power Network.

10

USE YOUR HANDS. Look for ways to be your own power source. The physical effort won't hurt, and you can cut down on some of those unnecessary electric gadgets. Remember, carbon is released in manufacturing, transportation to the store, and generating electricity.

Just because somebody came up with the idea of selling a battery-powered, self-lighting pepper mill doesn't mean you need one. The same goes for electric corkscrews. You can whip cream, brush your teeth and make foamy milk for your cappuccino manually. Stronger wrists just might help your tennis game.

11

BE A GREEN SPORT. Almost everybody needs to get more exercise. Why not go for a jog or a bicycle ride right from your front door instead of taking the car to a gym? Football consumes less energy than NASCAR. And isn't "motor sports" an oxymoron anyway? Maybe it's time to ask if car and motorcycle racing make sense in a warming world.

12

EAT FROM THE SEA. Fish, mussels, crab, and other seafood are excellent sources of high-value protein. Enjoy the bounty of the sea (and lakes, and rivers). But give it some thought, too, because a there are more than a few environmental issues surrounding fish and shellfish.

Industrialized fishing is a threat to many species, so take it easy on cod, tuna, shark, and halibut. If you're unsure which fish are sustainably managed, keep Environmental Defense's handy wallet-sized Seafood Selector on hand.

Some fish are known to concentrate environmental poisons such as mercury and pesticides. That's why the Environmental Protection Agency advises women who may become pregnant or are pregnant or nursing as well as children against eating certain types of fish. Which fish is right for you from an environmental point of view depends to a large extent on where you live. Talk to people at your local fish counter and find out what they think is the best local choice. See if your local shop offers eco-labeled fish, such as that certified by the Marine Stewardship Council.

With its rich maritime traditions and proximity to fisheries, the United States is blessed with excellent choice in seafood. So do Americans really need to eat fish sticks from whitefish caught far from shore, frozen at sea, shipped to China, thawed, processed, re-frozen, then shipped to the US? Probably not.

PLAY IT AGAIN, SAM: RECYCLE. Unsorted trash is a gigantic environmental problem as well as an economic cost paid through your taxes. Separated trash, on the other hand, is an economic resource.

Recycling an aluminum container saves 95 percent of the energy required to make a new one. An 11-watt low-energy lightbulb can run for 33 hours on the energy saved by recycling a single plastic PET bottle. A ton of recycled paper saves 17 trees (and we need those trees to process our excess carbon).

So get in the habit of sorting plastic, metal, glass, paper, and batteries. Old paint, chemicals, oil, electronics, and appliances should be taken to the proper facilities for disposal.

14

BUY LARGER QUANTITIES. Packaging waste accounts for fully one-quarter of everything that goes in the trash, and most of that can be recycled. But even better from the perspective of resources and energy is to avoid bringing excess packaging home from the store in the first place. Look for refillable containers whenever you shop. If you can't find them, ask to talk to the store manager.

DON'T TOSS BATTERIES. There's been great success in the effort to promote battery recycling by the manufacturers of lead-acid batteries, which are used in motor vehicles. With help from consumers and retailers, the industry recycled 99.2 percent of used battery lead from 1999 to 2003. That makes the lead-acid battery the nation's most highly recycled consumer product.

But the numbers don't look so impressive when it comes to recycling of other batteries. With only one in six North American households recycling non-vehicle batteries, US residents throw about 179,000 tons of batteries into the trash every year. Because batteries disposed of in landfills and incinerators can put significant amounts of toxic substances into the air and water, battery waste prevention and recycling strategies are critical. So buy products that minimize battery use, choose rechargeables where appropriate, and check with your solid local waste department for advice on proposal disposal of old batteries.

16

KEEP YOUR GARDEN GREEN. If we can't apply environmental principles around our own homes, how we can expect farmers to think ecologically?

Do you really need pesticides and herbicides? Look at what you have in the garden shed and see if there's a better alternative. In the US, home and garden applications account for more pesticide use per acre than agriculture.

Have a look at your machines. Do you really need all these noisemakers? Is it possible to take care of your garden with hand tools?

If you need a power mower, choose an electric model. If that isn't practical, a four-stroke emits less pollution and runs quieter than a two-stroke. By using a 10 percent blend of ethanol-enriched fuel, you can help lower greenhouse gas emissions by as much as 30 percent. The reductions are even greater when using blends with more ethanol.

Irrigate with rainwater, and water at sunset, when you won't lose so much to evaporation. Try to use a hose rather than sprinklers; otherwise you may waste everything you've saved with low-flow toilets and showers.

Try just changing your attitude. One person's overgrown garden is another person's haven for butterflies, birds, chipmunks and other wildlife. Try to save a patch of nettles in your garden. You don't have to go near them, but butterflies love them. The mother butterfly lays her eggs on the underside of the nettle leaf, and when the caterpillar emerges the leaf provides essential nutrition. Those caterpillars will attract beautiful birds into your garden.

A hammock is just about the most environmentally sound addition imaginable for your garden.

Consider what's important to you. Do you want a tidy show garden, full of non-native plant species, or do you prefer a patch of wild nature? Beauty, after all, is in the eye of the beholder.

17

GIVE LIVING PLANTS. American consumers spend more than $5 billion every year on cut flowers and related floral items, and about two-thirds of that is for imported blooms. But it's not hard to find ways to cheer up our homes with floral color and scent and still avoid pesticides, artificial fertilizers, and air transportation. Next time you visit your local florist, look first at the potted plants. Your dinner host will be just as happy, and the gift will last much longer. Season permitting, you might even put out a little extra effort and make your own bouquet of local wildflowers.

Be careful not to trespass when picking flowers and never take them from a nature reserve or protected site without permission. Untended roadsides and public rights of way are often good sources of wildflowers.

THINK ABOUT YOUR DRINK. After acquiring a reputation for inferiority some years ago, ecologically produced wines and beers have made dramatic improvements. Vineyards in warm climates have done the best job of cutting out chemical pesticides, probably because the fungi that attack grapes prefer damp environments. A Google search on "organic wine" will get hundreds of hits from producers all over the world. Also on the web, BeerTown.org features a brewpub locator to help you find your local craft brewer.

19

DEMAND BETTER TRAIN CONNECTIONS. Too few of us travel America by train. And no wonder: the best Amtrak ticket from New York to Los Angeles requires fifty-four hours and costs $165. For a little more than twice that much, you could fly direct in about eight hours.

Send an email to your Congressperson and ask why we don't have better high-speed trains and train connections.

SWITCH TO A GREEN CAR. Transportation-related carbon emissions account for about a third of all carbon dioxide emissions in the US, but carbon dioxide isn't the only hazard coming from our tailpipes. Each year the average auto emits almost 730 pounds of regulated pollutants, including carbon monoxide, nitrogen oxides, hydrocarbons, sulfur dioxide, and particulates. That's why switching to a greener car and more sustainable driving habits are among the best ways for individuals to drastically reduce their contribution to global warming and other air pollution.

Start by purchasing the most fuel-efficient and least-emitting model in the vehicle class that best meets your transportation needs. For help, consult the American Council for an Energy-Efficient Economy's Green Book®, which ranks all makes and models on fuel economy, emissions, and other measures. A growing number of Americans are turning to hybrid-electric vehicles, which increase fuel economy by as much as 80 percent. Drivers of diesel vehicles might consider using biodiesel or biodiesel fuel blends, which are produced from domestic, renewable sources.

You can also save fuel by avoiding aggressive driving habits and planning daily trips to combine errands and minimize the time your vehicle runs. Regardless of what kind of vehicle you drive, you'll conserve more fuel if you keep your wheels aligned, your tires properly inflated, and your engine tuned.

PLEASE (DON'T) STANDBY. Some of your appliances use up to half as much energy on standby as they do when they're in use. If you turn off your TV, clock radio, computer, and broadband connection when they aren't being used, you can save money and cut down on your contribution to global warming.

A plug-in electric meter helps you find out which appliances in your home are consuming the most energy, and can help you decide whether they should be turned off.

SWITCH IT OFF. The folk musician Arlo Guthrie once said, "You can't have a light without a dark to stick it in." So let empty rooms be dark rooms. And switching to modern, low-energy bulbs will save money as well as reducing your "carbon footprint." The new compact fluorescent bulbs cost more to buy, but they last about ten times longer than incandescents. Replacing a 100-watt standard incandescent with a 32-watt compact fluorescent can save at least $30 in energy costs over the life of the bulb. If every US household replaced one standard bulb with a compact fluorescent, we would prevent as much pollution as removing a million cars from the road.

23

WASH SMART. Avoid pre-washing and fabric softener, don't use more detergent than necessary, and choose environmentally friendly brands. Always wash a full load. And since about 90 percent of the energy used by washing machines is for heating the water, use lower temperatures when possible. Simply switching the setting from hot to warm can cut a load's energy use in half.

24

DISH IT OUT. Make sure the dishwasher is full (but not overloaded) before turning it on, use the economy setting, and turn off the auto-dry function. If your dishwasher has its own heating element, connect the incoming line to cold water so you won't be rinsing in hot. In warm climates, running the dishwasher at night avoids adding heat and humidity to your house when the air conditioner is working hardest.

25

SAVE WATER. Don't let the tap run more than necessary, and if it's dripping, get it fixed. Check into low-flow toilets. If you're not in a position to replace your old full-flush toilet, check for leaks by adding food coloring to the tank; if there's a leak, color will appear in the bowl within 30 minutes. You could also place a weighted plastic half-gallon jug or a toilet dam in a conventional tank to displace and save water with each flush.

DRINK ORGANIC COFFEE. Organic coffee is not only better for your own well-being, but also the health of people in the world's coffee-growing regions. In Costa Rica alone, about 700 people fall acutely ill every year, and 30 die, from toxic pesticides that were banned long ago in the United States. Organic coffee plantations also follow more long-term, sustainable strategies for preserving biodiversity. US sales of organic coffee totaled about $89 million in 2005—up more than 40 percent over the previous year.

Other earth-friendly coffee designations include Fair Trade, which requires coffee growers to adhere to basic environmental management principles as well as labor and trade standards. Fair Trade also certifies tea, chocolate, and much more. Then there's the Bird Friendly® designation, which can be used only by growers who meet inspection and certification requirements of the Smithsonian Migratory Bird Center. While all Bird Friendly® coffees are also organic, not all Fair Trade products are.

LOVE YOUR SEWER. Let's admit it, most of us don't get all warm and fuzzy over the contents of our sewers. But they're not improved by adding paints, heavy metals, oils, solvents, or chemicals. If you find yourself pondering whether or not to flush something, keep in mind that treated sewage sludge is often used to fertilize fields for growing crops. Is it something you want to end up in your food chain?

Also remember that the toilet is no place to dispose of anything that it's not designed for, including cotton balls, cigarette butts, condoms, bandages, razor blades, tampons, or letters from the girl who broke your heart. All that flotsam and jetsam just makes the sewage treatment plant work harder.

28

MAKE YOUR OWN EARTH. It only takes a small outdoor space to set up your own compost bin, and taking the food waste out of your trash can cut by half the amount of garbage that has to be transported to a landfill. At the same time, you'll be making perfect soil for your potted plants or vegetable garden. If you don't have an outdoor space, think about investing in a worm composting system. This is a self-contained box into which you put your food waste and in return get a rich organic compost. Don't worry, the worms entertain themselves and they can't get out.

ATONE. You can compensate for your excess contribution to carbon dioxide releases. Here are three simple ways, though there are many more:

● Buy offsets to cover the carbon released when you travel by air. The money you spend will be used to fund your choice of carbon-reducing projects such as renewable energy, energy efficiency, and reforestation. For a consumers' guide to retail carbon offset providers, visit www.cleanair-coolplanet.org.

● Plant trees to absorb carbon. The average American family needs to plant 30 trees to offset the carbon dioxide produced by their daily energy use. To find out how many trees you need to plant in order to compensate for your own carbon emissions, visit American Forest's Climate Change Calculator at www.americanforests.org.

● Support projects aiming to replace fossil fuels with renewables. That can be anything from windmill electric generators to subsidies for solar ovens in the developing world.

SUPPORT THE CLEAN WATER RESTORATION ACT. In 1972, Congress passed the Clean Water Act, one of the most important environmental laws in the United States. It aimed to halt releases of large amounts of toxic pollution to waterways and to ensure surface waters are safe for human sports and recreation. In recent years, though, a series of Supreme Court decisions and administrative actions has repealed protections under the law for as much as 60 percent of the nation's waters and as many as 20 million acres of wetlands.

In response, some federal lawmakers have sponsored the Clean Water Restoration Act, a bipartisan measure that reaffirms Congress's intent to protect all the streams, wetlands, ponds, and rivers throughout the country from unregulated pollution. The Act doesn't create any new regulatory burdens, but simply restores the nation's clean water laws to where they were before the recent rollback by using the same longstanding definitions that guided enforcement during the 1970s, 1980s and 1990s.

Powerful economic interests can be expected to make their views known during the legislative process. People whose sole agenda is a healthy water environment for generations to come should be at the table, too.

31

LEAVE THE MUSKY SCENT TO OXEN. Natural musk, a glandular extract from musk oxen, beavers and musk deer, has long been used in medicine and perfumes.

As the price of natural musk has skyrocketed in recent decades, the cosmetics industry has almost completely converted to synthetic compounds containing muscone, the active ingredient. The same chemicals are widely used in soaps and fabric softeners, leading to increased levels in aquatic environments. While the health impacts of synthetic musk are not yet confirmed, there is concern that it affects estrogen production, and may be bad for humans as well as fish.

32

AVOID BROMINATED FLAME RETARDANTS. These compounds are linked to behavioral, learning, and reproductive disturbances. Like the infamous and now-banned PCBs and DDT, brominated flame retardants are easily absorbed by organisms of all kinds and very slow to break down in the environment. They are found in electronics, clothing, and furniture—ask before you buy!

In 2004, Europe banned two formulations of polybrominated diphenyl ether, a brominated flame retardant known to result in human exposure, and their use was discontinued in the United States in 2005. But around that time, scientists began finding alarming concentrations of the chemicals in ordinary Americans' bodies, including breast milk levels 10 to 20 times higher than in European mothers. The US Environmental Protection Agency is working with industry, environmental, and public health advocates, and other federal agencies, states, and nations to research potential health risks.

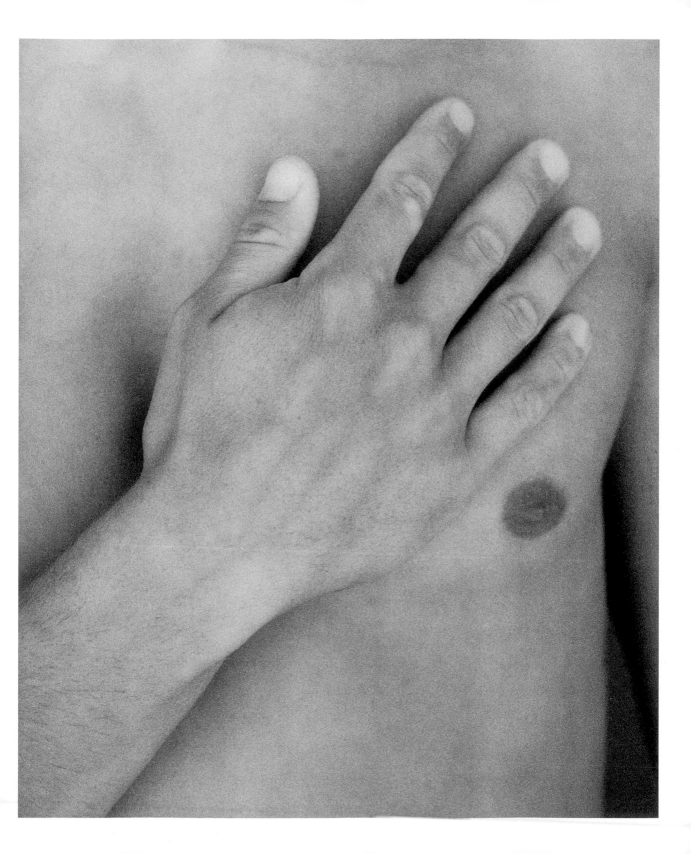

33

LET THE MERCURY FALL. For every degree you lower the heat or raise the cooling over eight hours, you can save one percent on your heating bill. In the average single-family home, going from 72°F to a still-comfortable 68° would reduce carbon dioxide production by 140 tons per year and save more than 20 percent on heating costs. Wear a pair of slippers and maybe a sweater and you'll never even notice the difference.

34

DON'T LET THE MERCURY OUT. Mercury is a highly toxic environmental pollutant that can cause severe brain damage, especially in children. As an element, it cannot be broken down by natural processes.

In 1998, the American Hospital Association signed an agreement with the Environmental Protection Agency in which it committed to eliminating mercury from the hospital waste stream. Many health care facilities are phasing out the use of mercury-containing thermometers and blood-pressure devices for safer alternatives, and families should follow suit. Contact your local household hazardous waste collection facility for disposal information.

Most batteries are mercury-free these days, though many button batteries used in cameras, watches, hearing aids, and other small devices still contain mercury. Make sure these are disposed of properly, and watch out for things like thermometers, circuit-breakers, and electrical switches.

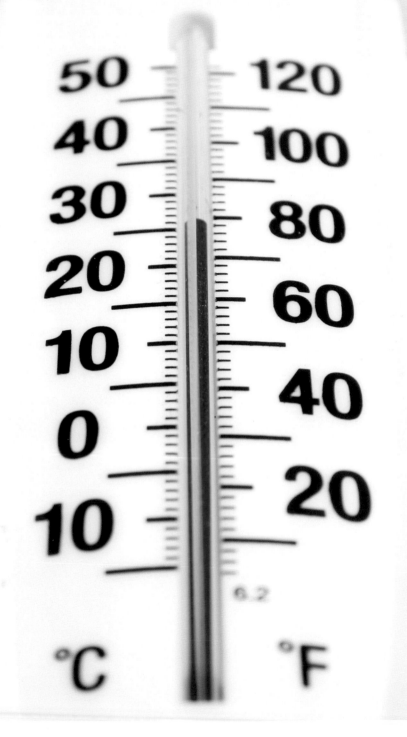

PROTECT YOUR CHILDREN. A recent study of personal care products found that children are exposed to an average of 61 different chemical ingredients every day, and that on average 27 of these ingredients have not been found safe for children by the government or the cosmetic industry's expert safety panel. Environmental Working Group offers a free Safety Guide to Children's Personal Care Products that can help you figure out what to avoid and what to use instead (www.cosmeticsdatabase.com). Also remember that cloth diapers are still best for your baby, for the environment, and for your budget. You can save several hundred dollars during those first three years, and even more if you have another child.

36

BE ANTI-ANTIBACTERIAL. Not all bacteria are bad, and it's possible to make your home "too clean." We've always lived with bacteria all around us, and your child's immune system needs to be stimulated by some exposure to bacteria in order to be healthy enough to defend against those really aggressive ones that might make her sick.

When the label brags that a product kills 99.9 percent of bacteria, think about that .1 percent. They survive and reproduce, and they're turning into resistant strains that are causing new environmental hazards. Antibacterial agents are being added to everything from toothpaste and dishcloths to socks and sports clothing. One company has even released a line of antibacterial pencils. Have you ever seen a sick pencil?

It's unnecessary. If you're not performing surgery, good old-fashioned hygiene and simple soaps do just fine.

37

KEEP ON ROLLIN'. The right pressure in your car's tires reduces fuel consumption. In fact, underinflating your tires by 15 percent results in a 2.5 percent drop in miles per gallon, increasing your vehicle's carbon dioxide emissions.

Next time you have to buy new tires, look for greener brands. The ordinary models in use on most cars contain cancer-causing oils that wind up in the environment as the tire wears down, but some companies are now manufacturing alternatives that use citrus oils instead, reducing the use of petroleum products in tires by as much as 80 percent.

STICK TO THE SPEED LIMIT. Fuel consumption—and accompanying greenhouse gas emissions—increases by about 30 percent as your speed goes from 50 to 70 miles per hour. And then it increases by 60 percent when you go from 70 to 90 mph. Lower driving speeds also save lives.

39

EAT WITH THE SEASON. Local, seasonal food requires less energy to grow and transport. It's generally less expensive than food that is scarcer or has traveled a long way, and it tends to be fresher, tastier, and more nutritious.

To find out what's in season where you live, visit your local farmers' market.

40

EAT YOUR VEGETABLES. Your mother was right, but perhaps not for the same reasons we're talking about here. It takes 68 calories of fossil fuel to produce one calorie of pork and 35 calories of fuel to make one calorie of beef. Eating lower down on the food chain requires less energy. It's better for the planet if you eat soybeans rather than animals raised on soybeans. It's not necessary to become a vegetarian, but you might try one meatless dinner a week.

In addition to energy use, livestock farming causes other problems. One is the destruction of rainforests to make space for grazing land, which reduces biodiversity and kills off big, carbon-absorbing trees. Another is the amount of methane produced by cattle, goats, and sheep. Methane is a powerful greenhouse gas—its effect is up to 25 times as damaging as carbon dioxide. The animals we eat produce more greenhouse gases than the entire transportation sector—an incredible 18 percent of the worldwide total.

From an environmental perspective, chicken is a better alternative than red meat for animal protein.

41

PLAN YOUR SHOPPING. Try to avoid unnecessary trips to the store in your car. On average, the food we eat has traveled 50 percent further than it did just 20 years ago. Much of this is due to increased imports of food—and there's no denying that variety, freshness and quality are improved by transport networks. But half of the total carbon dioxide load generated by food—from farm to table—comes at the consumer end, mainly in getting it home from the store.

There's a big difference in environmental impact between transporting food in fully loaded trucks and carrying a couple bags in the trunk of your car.

42

COMMUTE SMART. Private car travel accounts for more than half of all carbon dioxide emissions from the transportation sector, and daily commuting to jobs and school generates most of that. That's a good place to start looking for ways to conserve energy.

Public transportation is far better. Ride a bike or walk if you can. A 15-mile round-trip commute to work each day amounts to about 5,000 miles per year. If you drive a car that gets 25 mpg, your annual commute produces almost two tons of carbon dioxide. That's the equivalent of flying from New York to Los Angeles—twice.

4.3

PLANT TREES. By making a contribution to a tree-planting project, you can help restore a rainforest or stop desert sands from claiming more productive land. According to the US Department of Agriculture, an acre of forest absorbs six tons of carbon dioxide, while the net cooling effect of a young healthy tree is equivalent to 10 room-size air conditioners operating 20 hours a day.

By planting trees, you're shaping a better future.

4.4.

REFUSE DIRECT ADVERTISING. A huge amount of trees, ink and energy are wasted in printing and distributing direct-mail advertising that goes straight from the mailbox to the trash. If you read the ads, great. If you don't, check out the Center for a New American Dream's Junk Mail Campaign for tips on getting off the lists. That will be about 100 pounds a year that you don't have to carry out to the recycling bin.

BE ECO-CHIC. It's time to take a fresh look at the term ecological, which, let's face it, has acquired a ring of self-righteous finger-wagging. Ecological thinking is no longer a list of don'ts seemingly aimed at making life boring. Looking at your personal impact on the web of life can open doors to fulfilling experiences and meaningful change.

You don't have to live in a commune and eat lentil soup at every meal. Ecology has actually become chic, even trendy, and is fuel for some great cocktail-party chatter. Check out eco-resorts, eco-sports, eco-holidays, eco-pets, eco-homes, eco-design, eco-furniture, eco-art and eco-weddings.

AVOID PLASTIC. To be sure, plastic is the only choice for many uses. It's light, strong, flexible, waterproof and inexpensive. But many plastics are associated with chemical pollution, both in manufacturing and in final disposal. PVC plastics are among the worst offenders, because they usually contain softeners (called phthalates) which have been shown to cause cancer, disrupt hormone function, and affect the liver and reproductive organs. PVC products are marked with a triangle and the number 3. They're found in a wide range of products and packaging materials.

Plastics are manufactured mainly from petroleum and natural gas, and that means they contribute to the greenhouse effect.

Where possible, buy environmentally sound goods made from glass, leather, wood, cotton, or wool. They feel nicer, last longer, and age better.

ENJOY A BARBECUE. But avoid lighting the charcoal with toxic petroleum distillates. Instead, use a chimney starter—an up-right metal tube with a heatproof handle and a wire partition in the center. Just put a few sheets of newspaper in the bottom and the briquettes in the top, and light the paper with a match.

Charcoal isn't really the best use of timber—an acre of forest can produce only about one-tenth as much charcoal as timber. Fortunately, it doesn't take a great deal of charcoal to feed your barbecue.

Gas grills contribute to global warming (charcoal is carbon neutral), but they also burn cleaner. Gas is preferable to electricity.

SIT PRETTY. Choose outdoor furniture made from wood or cast iron rather than plastic. Look for products made from American alder or cedar instead of buying tropical woods that have been transported halfway round the world. If you do buy tropical woods, make sure your tables and benches come with an eco-label, such as the Forest Stewardship Council certification. That certainly reduces the likelihood that you'll be contributing to the destruction of rainforests.

DRINK TAP WATER. While sales of bottled water have exploded in recent years, water from bottles is not necessarily cleaner or safer than water from the tap.

The United States has one of the safest water supplies in the world, and public water suppliers must provide an annual report to customers on drinking water quality. Those reports are available from the water supplier or by visiting the Environmental Protection Agency's website at www.epa.gov.

Still, the United States leads the world in total consumption of bottled water, at more than 25 billion liters. If people are drinking bottled water as an alternative to sugary fizzy drinks, that's probably a good thing for public health. But if your tap water is just as good, why pay a thousand times as much for water that contributes to global warming?

SAVE IN THE KITCHEN. The federal government's ENERGY STAR certification program aims to help consumers make wiser choices about the appliances they purchase. With the help of ENERGY STAR, Americans saved enough energy in 2006 alone to avoid greenhouse gas emissions equivalent to those from 25 million cars—while saving $14 billion on their utility bills.

But there's no need to switch before your current machines are at the end of their useful life. A lot of resources and energy go into making appliances.

While you're waiting, make sure you regularly vacuum the coils on the back of the fridge so the compressor won't need to work as hard to maintain a low temperature. Defrosting also cuts the load on the compressor, as does letting warm food cool to room temperature before putting it in to chill.

51

CONTACT A COMPANY. Take the time to call or email a customer service department. Ask questions about the contents of their products, as well as their manufacturing practices, packaging, and transportation.

Companies are very careful to track these statistics, and nothing is more effective at changing corporate behavior than consumer pressure.

52

ASK QUESTIONS. Do you own stocks? Use your right to get answers from management at annual shareholder meetings. Be concrete: Has the company looked into hybrids for its car fleet or delivery vehicles? Is there a plan to balance carbon emissions? Has the company achieved ISO 14001 environmental certification?

Management is obliged to answer these questions, and to make their replies available for shareholders who don't attend the meeting, usually by posting questions and answers on the corporate website.

53

SUPPORT RESPONSIBLE COMPANIES. Most large companies—and many small and mid-sized enterprises—publish corporate environmental reports. These may be anything from a brief statement on a website to thorough documentation printed and distributed to shareholders along with the company annual report.

54

USE THE INTERNET. Download music. Legal downloads are less expensive than CDs. Less energy and resources are consumed by downloading than by pressing and distributing physical CDs.

The same goes for newspapers, magazines, catalogs, and audiobooks. Even films, if you have a newer computer and a broadband connection.

But a good book should still be read on paper. For the time being at least, no computer monitor can substitute.

55

USE THE LIBRARY. Borrowing books, CDs, and films is a resource-saving form of cultural recycling.

...ragmente

über

...mation.

Zur

...äuterung

des

...und vierten Bandes

des

...um's.

Von

...Rambach,

...tes Heft.

...und Stettin,

...Nicolai

CHECK YOUR CHEMICALS. Go through the products you use in the laundry, kitchen, and bathroom. Read the content labels, find out if they're harmful to the environment, and make a decision on whether you really need to be using them in your home.

THINK GLOBALLY, ACT LOCALLY (WITHIN REASON). If we were to blindly follow this simplistic bumper-sticker sentiment in our eating habits, we'd have to go back to living half the year on dandelion greens and acorn mush.

All else being equal, however, local food bought in season is a better choice than exotic foods shipped—or worse, flown—into the United States.

Hundreds of different varieties of apples are grown across the country. Look for a local variety—perhaps a Red or Golden Delicious, a Gala or McIntosh before picking out an apple from Argentina. Some products may take a few weeks longer to reach your store's shelves than the ones flown in from afar, but they're worth the wait.

That doesn't mean that food produced in the US is always the best environmental choice. A sun-ripened tomato from Mexico may require less energy than one grown in a hothouse here at home. A beef cow that has grazed in New Zealand might not use more resources than one raised on feed in Texas.

Perhaps you have a weakness for mangoes flown in from Haiti. Then you should eat your mangoes and be happy. But add the carbon dioxide for transportation—about five times the weight of the fruit—to your personal greenhouse gas calculation. Choose four pounds of a locally grown vegetable instead of four pounds of an imported variety and you're back to even.

SAVE A THREATENED SPECIES. Being a friend to wildlife isn't only a matter of caring about photogenic species with cute babies. In 2007, 607 animal species and 744 plant species were listed as threatened or endangered in the United States, and another 138 animal and 140 plant species were candidates for listing. All this points to wider—undesirable—environmental changes.

You can help conservationists inventory species in your area. For birdwatchers, Audubon and the Cornell Lab of Ornithology promote conservation through their annual Great Backyard Bird Count. Or see if there are local bird clubs or other wildlife groups in your area that take inventories. For more information about biodiversity efforts underway in your state, visit the Biodiversity Partnership online at www.biodiversitypartners.org.

EAT A THREATENED PIG. Paradoxically, some species are threatened because there is no market left for breeders. In the US today, 75 percent of pigs and 60 percent of beef cattle come from only three main breeds. Choose meat produced by a heritage breeder instead—pork chops from Red Wattle pigs, or steak from Dexter cattle—and you'll help that breed live on.

GIVE TO THE LESS FORTUNATE. Sometimes it requires a certain level of material well-being to be able to make positive environmental choices. Hundreds of millions of people around the world still live in such poverty that they would almost certainly consider a job in a polluting factory or on a plantation drenched in chemicals to be a blessing.

Fortunately, you already give to the less fortunate—when you pay taxes.

The US is the world's leading provider of economic aid to poor nations, and many of the poverty reduction projects supported by the Agency for International Development address environmental concerns including biodiversity, climate change and pollution prevention. Unfortunately, the US still has not met the UN target of donating at least 0.7 percent of national income to poor nations, giving only 0.22 percent of its income to the poor in 2005.

So keep helping the less fortunate improve the environment. Support the government's aid to developing countries, and encourage it to give even more generously—while at the same time giving to causes close to your heart.

PLAN YOUR CITY. Building suburbs and shopping centers on prime agricultural land may make economic sense today, but that doesn't mean it won't be seen as madness tomorrow. The more our cities and towns sprawl out, the more energy we use.

Land use planning processes are open to public input. Look to see what the comprehensive plan calls for in your area, and pay attention to proposed building projects. Have your say before construction begins, while there's still time to make changes and explore alternatives.

The Earth's population is expected to be 9 billion souls by the year 2050. Let the US be a model for building smart urban areas and saving our fields for growing food and biofuels.

FLY SMART. Unfortunately, air travel uses a lot of energy—and green fuels for airplanes aren't here yet. To be sure, the newer planes are more efficient than the older ones, but that savings is more than balanced by the overall growth in total air miles traveled.

Air traffic accounts for about 3 percent of total carbon dioxide releases worldwide. Many scientists believe the global warming effects are greater because that carbon is released at high altitudes.

But the opportunity to leave behind winter for a sunny beach with a few hours in the air is just too enticing for many. And there's no need to give up on such luxuries if you make an attempt to balance your lifestyle with some fairly painless sacrifices elsewhere.

Don't drive more than you need to. Step up to a green car or ride a bike to work. Shop for what you need, not as a form of therapy. Then you can treat your family to that holiday some place warm and exotic. Just don't waste your "carbon quota" on other things that you can easily do without.

Like sitting still in traffic every day.

ENJOY YOUR PLEASURE BOAT. Just don't let your marine behavior add to pollution. Sailing or rowing is of course preferable to tearing up the water in a motorboat. If you do buy a motorboat, four-stroke engines are a better environmental choice than two-strokes, where almost a third of the fuel goes unburned into the water.

Look for an eco-label on any hull paint you use. Toxins from hull paint are released over time, especially during underwater hull cleaning. They may be absorbed by mussels and worms, and are then passed up the food chain to fish, birds and humans, posing health risks.

Carefully choose the products you use for bathing, dish-washing and laundry on or near the water. And always wait until you come to a harbor with proper sewage disposal before emptying your toilet tank.

64.

COMPARE ELECTRICITY CONSUMPTION. Appliances may look alike and offer the same features, but differ a lot in the amount of energy they use. Try to choose the ones that use less. A plasma TV can pull twice as much current as an LCD in the same size. And a few extra inches in size can mean a big increase in electricity use.

65

COMPARE MORE. Choose a greener computer. The federal ENERGY STAR program certifies computers, while the Silicon Valley Toxics Coalition offers a report card rating brands on environmental and other measures.

Ask questions when you're shopping, and press for good answers. When manufacturers hear from their retail partners that consumers are asking about environmental features, they are spurred into taking action.

Greenpeace maintains an excellent "Guide to Greener Electronics" that ranks manufacturers on a range of issues, from chemicals and recycling to "global policies and practices." Go to www.greenpeace.org/international/ campaigns/toxics/electronics/how-the-companies-line-up.

DRESS GREEN. Some outdoor clothing is treated with fluorine-based chemicals to repel water while allowing moisture from your body to get out. That's a great feature, but there are alternatives to fluorine, which may impact the health of workers in the manufacturing chain.

If you already own this type of clothing, there's no reason to throw it out, but if you re-treat it, use a fluorine-free durable water repellent.

When you're shopping, look for ecological waterproofing. And natural materials like cotton, wool, and leather often do the job just as well as synthetics. After a shipwreck in 1915, Sir Ernest Shackleton and the crew of the Endurance spent 17 months in Antarctica dressed in gabardine wool.

How long are you planning to be outdoors?

AVOID DRY CLEANING. Despite the name, there's nothing "dry" about dry cleaning. Your clothes are immersed in a solvent, usually perchloroethylene—also known as PERC—which is associated with unpleasant nervous system effects ranging from dizziness, fatigue, and headaches to loss of muscular coordination and even unconsciousness. PERC also contributes to depletion of the ozone layer.

The best solution is, of course, to buy clothes that you can wash yourself. But some dry cleaners are beginning to use much more benign solvents, including liquid carbon dioxide—which doesn't contribute to global warming, since the carbon is removed from the air in the first place.

SHARE A CAR. It won't necessarily mean that the total mileage you drive will be less, but that will probably be the case. It certainly requires less energy to manufacture and maintain one car instead of two. And it's less expensive as well. With the money you save, it might be possible to upgrade to a green car.

According to a recent analysis, the number of new solo drivers in the US grew by almost 13 million from 1990 to 2000. By joining a car-sharing network, you get to reserve a vehicle whenever you need one and pay only per trip, while ride sharing matches up car owners with passengers who usually make a contribution toward fuel costs.

Similarly, you might consider joint ownership of a boat or lawn mower with a friend or neighbor.

SEND A LETTER TO YOUR LOCAL NEWSPAPER. Letters to the editor are among the most read pages of the newspapers. In addition to helping shape public opinion, you might encourage politicians to follow their best instincts and support effective policies. See if you can encourage incentives for expanding the number of gas stations offering green fuels, perhaps through reduced taxes. Support your local government's recycling efforts, or construction of wind power plants, or something else close to your heart.

Next, go online and send the same letter to relevant blogs.

70

BE A GOOD BUILDER. Natural materials are preferable to synthetics, which can cause environmental problems in manufacturing and may even be hazardous to occupants' health. Before you choose building materials, find out where they come from and how far they have been transported. Be especially careful about threatened tropical woods.

Use of chromated copper arsenate to pressure-treat timber against fungi and insects is now restricted in the United States, though CCA-treated products are still available. CCA is unpleasant stuff for you, your kids, and the environment. Alternatives are available. You may still find old railroad ties or telephone poles impregnated with creosote and be tempted to use this timber for outdoor projects. Don't.

71

SAVE AT HOME. More than 20 percent of US energy use is in dwellings, and almost half of that goes to space and water heating. That means there are big carbon savings to be found right where you live.

Start with attic insulation. Simply adding a layer of 10-inch thick insulation will save a lot of energy and money.

Wall insulation is another very cost effective way of reducing heat loss. Uninsulated cavity walls lose more heat than any other part of your home and could be costing you an extra $500 a year in wasted energy. Retrofitting uninsulated walls involves drilling small holes and injecting fiber, foam, or other material. For tips on choosing and installing the insulation right for your home, see the US Department of Energy's Energy Efficiency and Renewable Energy website at www.eere.energy.gov.

72

BE HEALTHY. When you get right down to it, your health isn't only your own business. If you get sick, you have to get treatment, and the health care industry consumes enormous resources. Minding your health frees up care for those who may need it more.

So watch what you eat, take walks every day—or bike, go to a gym, play tennis or basketball. Whatever you do, don't smoke. Besides coating your lungs with carcinogenic tar, tobacco farming takes agricultural land that could be used to grow food or biofuel.

73

RIDE A BICYCLE. Anytime it's possible. Let's say you have a five-mile commute to work. Cycling instead of driving will cut your carbon dioxide emissions by more than 1,300 pounds per year and save you as much as $1,000.

LOOK FOR THE ECO-LABEL. Don't believe that a brand is better simply because it's marketed as "green" or "natural." Look at the list of ingredients in food products or the power consumption of an appliance and make your own judgment.

Eco-labels to look for at the grocery store include US Department of Agriculture organic certified and Food Alliance certified, both of which guarantee more sustainable production methods. When buying seafood, consider the Marine Stewardship Council, Fishwise, or Seafood Safe labels.

Also, look for warning labels. If a product is a danger to the skin and eyes, or if it's poisonous, think carefully about whether you really need it in your home.

COTTON IS GREAT, BUT ... Industrialized cotton farming can cause some serious environmental impacts from artificial irrigation and excessive use of pesticides.

Until the 1960s the Aral Sea was the world's fourth-largest lake. Then Soviet central planners diverted its main rivers to irrigate huge farms growing cotton. At its worst, in the late 1990s, the Aral was down to just 25 percent of its original surface area and salinity had quadrupled, killing most native fish and plants. A restoration project is helping, but the situation is still dire.

As one of the world's top cotton producers, the US has also been impacted by related pesticide use, with massive fish kills triggered by runoff from sprayed fields, bird deaths from eating poisoned insects, and illnesses—and even deaths—among farmworkers. Look for organically farmed cotton clothing.

RELAX BY A FIRE. An open fireplace provides a cozy spot to curl up with a good book on a chilly winter day. But be aware that you might not be getting as much heat into the house as goes up the chimney.

You'll get the best thermal effect and least environmental impact if you burn split hardwood that has dried for a year or two outdoors under a rain shelter and a week or two indoors.

Never burn pressure-treated lumber, painted or glued wood, chipboard, plastic or trash, as these can produce fumes that are good neither for you nor your chimney.

A modern enclosed wood stove sacrifices some of the coziness but puts much more of the firewood's heat energy into the room.

BE COOL. Air conditioning can increase your car's fuel consumption by up to 10 percent. On the other hand, driving with the windows down causes drag that burns more fuel at higher speeds. So perhaps the best rule of thumb is to open a window in town and use the A/C on the highway.

Most cars with automatic climate control have a switch to manually turn off the A/C. But it's a good idea to turn it on once in a while to let the liquid coolant circulate. This keeps seals in the system from drying out and leaking.

Even when it's cold out, some automatic climate controls will go on to reduce humidity. Check to see whether this is the case in your car.

PAINT PRETTY. Paints can be of concern due to the toxic chemicals they contain. Volatile Organic Compounds (VOC) are the solvents and other chemicals in paint that evaporate during use. These can damage the environment and affect human health. You can help reduce the impact of paint on the environment by choosing products with a low VOC level—which are available nowadays at most major home improvement stores. Consider using water-based products when staining wood.

Some solvents in glues have also been found to be highly toxic and pose a risk to the environment, wildlife, and human health. When purchasing strong adhesives, try to buy water-based, solvent-free glues and keep them away from children at all times.

CLEAN THE OLD-FASHIONED WAY. Many of the cleaning products for sale in your local supermarket contain harmful chemicals. Chances are, you don't need more than dishwashing soap and a general-purpose cleaner.

Try cleaning the way your grandmother did. Vinegar or lemon juice work fine on the toilet and tiles. Vinegar removes stains and dishwashing liquid cleans windows. Make your oven shine again by painting the inside with a solution of simple liquid soap and leaving it for an hour or so at low heat. Spills on stuffed furniture can be attacked with baking powder in warm water.

80

CHANGE YOUR HAIRSTYLE. A test of 38 different gels, sprays and mousses uncovered a lot of bad news for health and the environment.

All the tested hair products contained chemicals known or believed to be allergenic, carcinogenic, mutagenic, or disruptive to the hormonal and reproductive systems. The amounts used are so small that the danger is minimal, but chemical exposure is always a greater concern for young people.

81

CHANGE YOUR MAKEUP. This isn't so easy. There are plenty of soaps, shampoos, conditioners and shower gels that claim to have botanical and other natural ingredients, but it's a lot harder to find truly green cosmetics.

At a minimum, try to simply choose products with fewer ingredients. If you find a cream with 27 different chemicals that you can't pronounce, chances are some of them will be things that you and the environment can do without.

BUY CERTIFIED ORGANIC. An "organically grown" guarantee lets you know that you're bringing home healthier food. As the Children's Health Environmental Coalition says, "By purchasing organically grown foods, we support more than a line of safer food products. We also work to create a just and sustainable food system for ourselves and for future generations."

A certified organic farm won't pollute lakes and rivers with pesticides that wind up on our plates when we eat fish. Certified banana plantations aren't sprayed against weeds, insects, and fungi; conventional growers spray as much as 100 pounds of various poisons every year.

An easy choice? Not always.

There's a strong case for the industry argument that artificial fertilizers and pesticides are essential to feeding the world's burgeoning population. Just look at the tripling in global grain production between 1950 and 2000, as land devoted to these crops grew by just 10 percent. Organic farms generally produce less per acre, and if everyone ate organic we'd be forced to have much more land under the plow, limiting biodiversity and causing other environmental problems. But markets work, and demand for organic food leads to improved production methods and higher yields.

Organic farmers are commonly seen as fuzzy-headed dreamers. But perhaps it's worth putting at least some of your food budget into the hands of visionaries with an explicit ethical agenda, at the expense of the cold calculations of global agribusiness.

Easy or not, it's your choice.

STUDY CHEMISTRY. There are more chemical compounds in the average home today than there were in the average laboratory a century ago. The flow of chemicals through our homes, workplaces, and natural surroundings is one of the most serious environmental threats we face. Cancer-causing PCBs are found in fish, meat contains flame retardants, cheese has traces of plastic softeners, and wild game is tainted with organic chlorine compounds from pesticides. The list goes on.

Back in 1976, Congress passed the Toxics Substance Control Act (TSCA) authorizing the Environmental Protection Agency (EPA) to control chemicals that pose an unreasonable risk to human health or the environment. Unfortunately, a 2006 Governmental Accountability Office study found that the EPA had reviewed only 200 of the 62,000 chemicals that were in commerce when the EPA first began reviewing substances under TSCA.

The EPA launched a program where chemical companies voluntarily provide test data on high production-volume materials, but the GAO found problems with it—including the chemical industry's refusal to provide data for more than 200 substances with high production volumes. Environmental advocates say TSCA has failed to protect people from unsafe chemicals, and have issued calls for reforms. Encourage your representatives in Washington to heed them.

CONSUME LESS. All due respect for low energy lamps, eco-certifications, ENERGY STAR appliances and Fair Trade coffee, but we can all do more to lessen our personal impact on poor Mother Earth.

The first step is to recognize that you can't reduce carbon emissions by going shopping, even at the right stores.

A good second step is to simply use less. Certain clothes, cars, and computers might use less resources than others, but more consumption always means more energy, natural resources, and pollution.

Everything you buy causes carbon emissions in manufacturing and transportation, and usually during use and final disposal as well.

Since 1993, a group called Adbusters has celebrated the last Saturday in November as "Buy Nothing Day," and the organizers claim it's now observed in more than 55 countries. It's fair to question the value of symbolic campaigns like this, but just pick a day and try to go 24 hours without spending any money. For most of us that's not easy, and making the effort can be an eye-opener.

85

FIX IT. "It's not worth sending back for repair." Heard that one before? Think twice the next time it comes up. We are individuals and families, not corporate machines forced to maximize profits to justify our existence. From a purely economic perspective, it may well not be worth $175 to repair a $200 gadget. But it might still be a wise environmental choice if the repair cuts out the energy and resources required to make a new one, and the old doesn't wind up on the trash heap just yet.

For some people, life is a competition to collect the most stuff. For others, personal satisfaction comes from leaving the world in slightly better shape than they found it. What kind are you?

Try to see the virtue in making old things work instead of constantly buying new ones.

86

USE USED. Anytime you can re-use something instead of buying a new item to replace it, you've done a good deed for the environment. Flea markets and auctions are always good sources for bargains, and the Internet is unparalleled for matching up buyers and sellers without wasting time on fruitless trips in the car.

SUPPORT WIND POWER. Wind is one of the biggest sources of new power generation in the US, where in 2007 total installed wind power capacity was over 11,600 megawatts (MW), enough to serve 3 million average households.

But the US lags behind the world's leading nation for wind power—Germany, which has more than 20,000 MW of wind energy capacity

As of 2007, the US still had no federal renewable electricity standard. That year Congress considered legislation that would require 15 percent of the country's electricity to come from renewable sources by 2020, but some European nations have set much more ambitious goals. They include Germany, which is aiming to be generating 27 percent of its electricity from renewable sources by 2020.

Encourage your representatives to be ambitious. And while the political process moves forward, look into installing your own windmill to pump water for the garden or generate electricity for a summerhouse or outdoor lighting.

WORK SMART. Small measures can add up to big improvements in your workplace. Switch to low-energy lightbulbs. Make double-sided copies. Get your company to switch to green cars. Cut business travel with videoconferencing. Recycle printer ink cartridges. Use bike messengers, or plan ahead so documents and samples can be sent by US Mail. Use recycled paper.

Go a step further and have your company perform a carbon audit, and then develop a concrete action plan for reducing greenhouse gas emissions.

Suggest that your IT department buy greener computers. Look around for appliances drawing electricity on stand-by. Computers, printers, coffee-makers, and copiers should be turned off completely when not in use.

Whenever possible, distribute internal information in .pdf format instead of printed on paper.

Suggest a program to certify your company or organization to the ISO 14001 environmental management standard.

89

DO YOUR HOMEWORK. If it's hard to choose between driving the car and taking the bus to work, maybe you should just stay home. If you have an office job, see if it's possible to devote a day every now and then to do paperwork, make phone calls and perform other tasks that you can do from the kitchen table.

Keep in mind that half of all the emissions our planet has to absorb come from job-related travel.

90

SIT LONGER. Check the materials that go into the sofa or stuffed chair you're considering that seems like such a great bargain: amide plastic resin, nylon, polyester, polyether foam, polypropylene, epoxy powder-coated steel, chromed steel, and viscose are all sources of considerable pollution in manufacture and disposal.

A more expensive model might have a completely different list of contents: beech or ash wood, leather, hemp, linen, horsehair, and cotton are generally better environmental choices. And the higher-priced furniture will likely age much better and be a better buy in the long run.

OBEY THE LAW. Our governments and agencies are home to many thoughtful, intelligent public servants who actually give a great deal of thought to their decisions. Politicians and bureaucrats at the national, regional, and local levels are (mostly) genuinely concerned and informed individuals working hard to protect the environment. Very few of our laws and regulations are created just to make your life more difficult.

The government certainly doesn't always get it right, and grand plans often fall victim to inadequate funding, staffing, or follow-through. But informed citizens making their views known can do a lot to break institutional inertia and get results.

The very nature of environmental regulation usually means inconvenience or higher costs for someone, somewhere. But the more we all feel that the burden is equally shared, the easier it is to do our part.

92

VENTILATE. During the winter, you need to let air into the house every now and then. But do it in short bursts rather than leaving a window slightly open all day. The best way is to turn down the heat, then open two windows and fill the house with fresh, cool air for a few minutes.

93

OBSERVE AND RESPECT. It's not just a cliché; you are indeed a part of nature. Don't just view the natural world through a window; don't let it be something you only visit now and then.

Take a trip to a national park or nature reserve. The next time you hear about development encroaching on the remaining untouched open space left in America, you'll have a clear idea what's being lost. Take a stand against poorly planned growth so your children and grandchildren will also have the opportunity to experience open, unpopulated nature.

When you get out in the woods or along a desolate coast, think about how you fit in. Observe and appreciate. A quiet walk with a backpack fills the senses far better than a motorized excursion.

DON'T LEAVE HOME WITHOUT YOUR MIND. If you travel abroad, don't just go on autopilot. Check with a travel agent or look online for websites on ecotourism. The concept is as much about economics as ecology, because true ecotourism will ensure that the money you spend on vacation benefits local people.

Look for green certified hotels, which will meet basic standards for sewage disposal, water conservation, energy management, and laundry procedures. Green hotels should also pay attention to the food served in restaurants and items sold in souvenir shops.

If you're planning a cruise, check to see if the ship runs on green fuel and is equipped with catalytic converters.

Put a little research into wildlife issues in the area you're planning to visit. The best protection for African gorillas, whales, and other creatures is when there is more money to be made bringing tourists to see them than there is in shooting them, or developing their habitats.

Make sure you don't buy souvenirs made from skins of threatened species.

Travel thoughtfully. Don't take anything home that should be left where it is, and don't leave anything that doesn't belong. The International Ecotourism Society (www.ecotourism.org) is a great resource for the environmentally aware traveler.

EAT VARIETY. That more than 80 percent of the world's spinach seed comes from Denmark may strike you as a banal factoid—especially if you hate spinach. But it's worth your interest, because it reveals the disturbing trend towards increasing monoculture, where the same species of plants are grown everywhere.

We need to strengthen biodiversity, where human activities support healthy ecological webs and landscape mosaics of agricultural land, lakes and streams, wetlands and forests. At the environmental summit meeting in Johannesburg in 2002, leaders of the world's governments adopted a UN convention calling for a reversal of biodiversity loss.

It's not enough to set aside reserves for threatened plant and animal species—and a spinach reservation would strike most of us as silly—but we can all help by "voting" for biodiversity with our food shopping choices. Look for different varieties of apples, tomatoes, lettuce and, yes, spinach.

GET THE KIDS OUTSIDE. Build a treehouse, go camping, boating, and hiking, make a bird box, plant bushes for your local butterflies, watch tadpoles turn into frogs in a pond in your garden. Or just find a stump and make it your own outdoor dining table. Get your family used to Sunday afternoons in the woods with a packed lunch.

Try to find a daycare where the children are outdoors as much as possible. Any time, any place teach your kids that nature is worth experiencing first-hand—and worth protecting for the future.

BE A ROLE MODEL. But don't overdo it. Avoid topics like "The energy required to produce all the world's dog and cat food ..." That will just turn off your pet-loving friends.

Instead, arm yourself with a collection of ohreallys. As in "Oh really? I didn't know that!"

- A single dripping tap can waste more than 6,000 gallons of water in a year, or enough for 400 showers.
- An average tree can absorb more than 25 pounds of carbon dioxide in a year, and at the same time produces enough oxygen for a family of four.
- One person who pees in a lake for one day will add enough nitrogen to feed a couple of pounds of algae.
- It takes 37 times as much energy to produce a couple of pounds of chocolate as it does to produce a couple of pounds of flour.
- Ten adults generate as much heat as a large radiator.
- A plastic bottle can remain in the ocean for 450 years.
- We are now using about 1,000 barrels of oil per second.
- Because they travel to the mainland by air, Hawaiian pineapples are among the most carbon intensive of foods, contributing about 40 pounds of carbon dioxide per pound of pineapple.

USE LESS. Don't start your teeth-brushing routine by applying so much toothpaste to your brush that three-fourths of it just ends up being wasted. Sure, it's insignificant (even if toothpaste costs more per pound than the better cuts of beef), but it helps to keep the right attitude. If the directions on the cleaning solution say to use a capful in a bucket of water, the floor won't get cleaner if you dump in a full cup. Your laundry won't get whiter from overdosing the detergent. Cut your living costs and save the planet at the same time.

When you cook, don't make so much you have to throw food away or let it grow mold in the back of the fridge. Instead, serve a smaller meal and then put out a fruit plate at the end of the meal so your family can eat a little more and still be a little healthier.

It all adds up to fewer resources for production, less energy for transportation and less waste to the landfill.

TRANSPORT LESS. Look around you. How many of the things in your house were made locally? It's not always easy to cut carbon dioxide by buying local. About 96 percent of all the clothing bought in the US is imported, for instance.

Another problem is that it's meaningless to compare distances alone, since the goods we buy are brought to us by different means of transportation. Take wine as an example. One study shows that a properly loaded container ship releases one-sixth as much carbon dioxide per pound as the most efficient trucks. So an environmentally aware New Yorker might have a cleaner conscience buying a nice piece of fruit shipped from Costa Rica rather than trucked from Mexico.

Another study says the difference is 13 times as much, so for Los Angelenos a ship from Central America would still beat the truck from south Florida.

But then along comes a third study showing that most shipping is inefficient, since many vessels still run on older diesel engines with no catalytic converters. In that case it's best to stick with the California zinfandel.

The truth is that it's almost impossible to know whether you're making the right choice from a transportation perspective. What is clear, however, is that it's worth supporting political leaders willing to take on powerful industries, such as by insisting that any carbon regulation program includes sea and air transport. Including transport in any carbon-trading regime would be a step towards letting market forces steer consumption habits in the direction of better environmental solutions.

CALL A POLITICIAN—AGAIN. Maker it clear that environmental issues make a difference in how you vote.

Such calls led some European cities to require solar heat in all new construction.

Such calls led Britain's prime minister to call for a 60 percent cut in carbon dioxide emissions by 2050.

Such calls led the governor of California to promise to "show the world that economic growth and the environment can coexist."

PRODUCTION FACTS

To produce this book with the least possible environmental impact, materials and business partners have been carefully selected.

This book is printed with soy-based ink on paper that has been harvested from well-managed forests with sustainable and environmentally sound practices. The text stock is Forest Stewardship Council (FSC) approved 140 gsm matt art paper produced by the Oji Paper Mill. The cover stock is FSC approved 400 gsm Esprime produced by PT Surya Pamenanang Mill. The binding uses non-animal sources for the adhesive.

FSC
Mixed Sources
Product group from well-managed
forests and other controlled sources

Cert no. SGS-COC-003843
www.fsc.org
© 1996 Forest Stewardship Council

PICTURE SOURCES

Figures refer to the hints in the main text. All images from Johnér picture agency, with the exception of those marked with an asterisk.

Front cover:
   Ryuichi Sato, Getty
   Images*
Back cover:
   Per Ranung
1 Photonica
2/3/4 Mats Widén
5 Peter Ahlén
6 Susanna Blåvarg
7/8 iStock Photo*
9 BrandX
10/11 Per Ranung
12 Hans Carlén
13/14 Jeppe Wikström
15 Per Ranung
16 Lena Granefelt
17/18 Karin Berglund/
   Naturbild
19 Per Ranung

20 Lars Thulin
21/22 Stefan Rosengren/
   Naturbild
23/24/25
   Mikael Dubois
26 Per Ranung
27/28 iStock Photo*
29 iStock Photo*
30 Jeppe Wikström
31/32 Philip Laurell
33/34 iStock Photo*
35/36 Ulf Huett Nilsson
37/38 iStock Photo*
39/40 Max Brouwers
41/42 Nicho Södling
43/44 Ewa Ahlin
45/46 Jeppe Wikström
47/48 Elliot Elliot
49/50 Per Ranung

51/52/53 Per Ranung
54/55 Mats Hallgren
56 Shutterstock*
57 Per Ranung
58/59 Workbook
60 David H Wells/Photonica
61 Image Source
62 Magnus Rietz
63 Jeppe Wikström
64/65 iStock Photo*
66/67 iStock Photo*
68/69 Per Ranung
70/71 Elliot Elliot
72/73 Mats Widén
74/75 iStock Photo*
76/77 Jeppe Wikström
78 Mats Hallgren
79 Per Ranung
80/81 L Ancheles

82 iStock Photo*
83 Per Ranung
84 Lars Thulin
85/86 Per Ranung
87 iStock Photo*
88 L Ancheles
89/90 Jeppe Wikström
91 iStock Photo*
92/93 Per Ranung
94 Image Source
95 Per Magnus Persson
96 Susanne Walström
97 Stefan Wettainen
98 Jeppe Wikström
99 Jeppe Wikström
100 Alexander Crispin

This book has been published with generous support from the following companies:

SEB   Securitas   AP Fastigheter

Advisory Board:

Georgia Destouni, Professor of Hydrology, Hydrogeology and Water Resources, Stockholm University, Sweden

Professor Andy Gouldson, Director of the Sustainability Research Institute at the University of Leeds, UK

Lennart Möller, Dr. Med., Professor of Health Risks in the Environment, Karolinska Institutet, Stockholm, Sweden

Natalie Suckall, Teaching and Research Assistant, School of Earth and Environment, University of Leeds, UK

Anders Wörman, Professor of River Engineering, The Royal Institute of Technology, Stockholm, Sweden

The power is in your hands.

You have the tools you need
to save the world.

The time to start is now.